The History of

Science

Disclaimer

The images included in this book are intended for illustrative purposes only. They are designed to enhance the reader's understanding and appreciation of the historical events and cultural elements discussed within the text. While every effort has been made to ensure the accuracy and authenticity of these images, they are artistic interpretations and may not represent exact historical details or realities.

The creators of this book have used a combination of historical references and creative liberties to produce these visual representations. As such, readers are encouraged to refer to primary historical sources and scholarly works for precise information.

Crafted by Skriuwer

Table of Contents

Introduction

Overview of the Significance of Science in Human History

Science has played a pivotal role in shaping human history, driving progress, and enhancing our understanding of the world around us. From ancient times to the present day, scientific inquiry has been a driving force in advancing human civilization in various ways.

One of the fundamental aspects of science is its role in expanding human understanding. Through systematic observation, experimentation, and analysis, science has enabled us to unravel the mysteries of the natural world and the universe. By studying the laws of nature and the principles governing the cosmos, scientists have been able to explain phenomena that were once considered supernatural or inexplicable. This quest for knowledge has broadened our horizons, deepened our understanding of the universe, and fostered a sense of curiosity and wonder about the world we inhabit.

Moreover, science has been instrumental in improving the quality of life for individuals and societies. Through scientific advancements in medicine, agriculture, technology, and engineering, we have been able to combat diseases, increase crop yields, develop innovative technologies, and enhance living standards. From the discovery of antibiotics to the development of vaccines, scientific breakthroughs have saved countless lives and alleviated suffering. Furthermore, advancements in communication, transportation, and infrastructure have connected people across the globe and facilitated the exchange of ideas and knowledge.

Additionally, science has been a driving force behind technological innovation and cultural progress. The application of scientific principles has led to the invention of revolutionary technologies that have transformed the way we live, work, and interact with the world. From the Industrial Revolution to the Information Age, science has fueled advancements in industry, communication, transportation, and entertainment. These technological innovations have not only improved efficiency and productivity but have also shaped the cultural landscape, influencing art, literature, and social norms.

Furthermore, science has played a crucial role in addressing societal challenges and promoting sustainability. By studying the impact of human activities on the environment and developing sustainable solutions, scientists have contributed to the preservation of ecosystems, the conservation of natural resources, and the mitigation of climate change. Through interdisciplinary research and collaboration, science has the potential to drive positive change and foster a more sustainable future for generations to come.

In conclusion, the significance of science in human history cannot be overstated. Its role in advancing human understanding, improving quality of life, driving technological innovation, and addressing global challenges is paramount. As we continue to explore the frontiers of scientific knowledge and push the boundaries of human ingenuity, science will remain a cornerstone of progress and a catalyst for positive change in the world.

Purpose and Scope of the Book

The purpose and scope of the book "The History of Science" are to provide a comprehensive and chronological narrative of the development of scientific knowledge from ancient times to the present day. By delving into the rich tapestry of human history, this book aims to showcase the pivotal role that science has played in advancing human understanding, improving the quality of life, and driving technological and cultural progress.

Throughout the chapters, readers will be taken on a journey through the annals of time, starting with the ancient beginnings of science where early humans used observational skills and rudimentary tools to understand their environment. The book then explores the scientific achievements of ancient civilizations such as Mesopotamia, Egypt, the Indus Valley, and China, highlighting their contributions to fields such as astronomy, mathematics, medicine, engineering, and urban planning.

As the narrative progresses, the reader will be introduced to key figures and advancements in classical science, including Euclid, Archimedes, and Ptolemy, as well as the Roman contributions to science and technology. The book also delves into the decline of classical science and the preservation of knowledge by Byzantine, Islamic, and monastic scholars.

Moving into the Islamic Golden Age, readers will learn about the translation movement and the House of Wisdom in Baghdad, as well as the significant contributions of figures like Al-Khwarizmi, Ibn Sina, and Alhazen in mathematics, astronomy, medicine, and optics. The narrative then transitions to medieval European science, discussing the Carolingian Renaissance, scholasticism, and the integration of Greek and Islamic science.

The book further explores the Renaissance and the Scientific Revolution, detailing the rediscovery of classical texts, the rise of humanism, and the groundbreaking work of figures like Copernicus, Galileo, Kepler, and Newton. It also examines the development of the scientific method and experimental science during this period.

The Age of Enlightenment, the Industrial Revolution, and the 19th and early 20th centuries are all covered, highlighting key advancements in various scientific disciplines and the establishment of scientific societies and academies. The narrative then leads into the mid to late 20th century, discussing the space race, developments in computer science, medical breakthroughs, and biotechnology.

The book concludes with a reflection on contemporary science and future directions, emphasizing modern advancements in physics, genetics, nanotechnology, and AI, as well as the role of science in addressing global challenges such as climate change and public health.

By providing this detailed and comprehensive exploration of the history of science, the book aims to inspire readers to appreciate the evolution of scientific knowledge and to contemplate the future of scientific discovery and its potential impact on society and the world at large.

Chapter 1

Ancient Beginnings

Early Observations and Natural Philosophies in Prehistoric Times

In the early stages of human history, long before the formal establishment of science as a discipline, our ancestors relied on keen observational skills and rudimentary tools to make sense of the world around them. This period, known as prehistoric times, marked the beginning of human curiosity and ingenuity in understanding natural phenomena. Early humans, living as hunter-gatherers in small communities, developed a deep connection with their environment and sought to unravel the mysteries of the natural world through direct observation and experimentation.

Observation played a crucial role in the lives of early humans as they navigated their surroundings, hunted for food, and adapted to changing environmental conditions. By closely observing the behaviors of animals, patterns in the sky, and changes in the landscape, early humans began to develop a rudimentary understanding of cause and effect in nature. For example, they observed the movement of celestial bodies to track time and seasons, which laid the foundation for the development of astronomy.

In addition to observational skills, early humans utilized simple tools and techniques to interact with their environment and improve their chances of survival. Tools such as sharpened stones, wooden spears, and fire allowed them to hunt more efficiently, build shelters, and cook food. Through trial and error, early humans honed their tool-making abilities and passed down knowledge from generation to generation, leading to the gradual refinement of techniques and tools.

Furthermore, early humans developed natural philosophies based on their observations and experiences, seeking to explain the natural phenomena they encountered. These early beliefs and philosophies laid the groundwork for the emergence of more structured forms of scientific inquiry in later civilizations. For example, early myths and stories about the origins of the world and the forces of nature provided a framework for understanding the natural world and our place within it.

Overall, the period of early observations and natural philosophies in prehistoric times represents the dawn of human scientific curiosity and exploration. By relying on keen observation, experimentation, and the development of rudimentary tools, early humans began to unravel the mysteries of the natural world and lay the foundation for the scientific advancements that would follow in later civilizations. This period highlights the innate human drive to understand and make sense of the world around us, a drive that continues to propel scientific inquiry and discovery to this day.

Contributions of Ancient Civilizations

Ancient civilizations played a pivotal role in laying the foundation for the development of science and technology that continues to shape our world today. In this section, we will delve into the scientific achievements of four key ancient civilizations: Mesopotamia, Egypt, the Indus Valley, and China.

Mesopotamia, often referred to as the cradle of civilization, made significant contributions to astronomy and mathematics. The Babylonians, for instance, developed a sophisticated system of astronomy that included the division of the sky into constellations and the creation of the first known written astronomical records. They also made advancements in mathematics, particularly in the development of the sexagesimal system, which laid the groundwork for modern concepts of time and geometry.

Moving to Egypt, this ancient civilization excelled in medicine and engineering. Egyptian physicians demonstrated advanced knowledge of human anatomy and surgical techniques, as evidenced by the Edwin Smith Surgical Papyrus, one of the oldest known medical texts. In the field of engineering, the construction of monumental structures such as the pyramids and temples showcased the Egyptians' mastery of architectural principles and engineering techniques that have stood the test of time.

The ancient Indus Valley civilization, known for its well-planned cities and sophisticated urban infrastructure, made remarkable advancements in urban planning and metallurgy. The cities of Harappa and Mohenjo-Daro featured a grid layout with organized streets, drainage systems, and public baths, reflecting a high level of urban planning and civic organization. Additionally, the Indus Valley people were skilled metallurgists, producing intricate artifacts in copper, bronze, and other metals, indicating a deep understanding of metallurgical processes.

In China, ancient scholars made significant contributions to astronomy, medicine, and engineering. Chinese astronomers developed a calendar system based on astronomical observations and calculations, leading to accurate predictions of celestial events. In the field of medicine, the Chinese excelled in herbal medicine, acupuncture, and diagnostic techniques that are still practiced today. Moreover, Chinese engineers pioneered innovations such as the invention of papermaking, the compass, and advanced hydraulic engineering systems like the Grand Canal.

Overall, the scientific achievements of ancient Mesopotamia, Egypt, the Indus Valley, and China laid the groundwork for the development of scientific knowledge and technological advancements that continue to shape our world today. These civilizations demonstrated a deep curiosity about the natural world, a commitment to empirical observation, and a drive to innovate and improve the quality of life for their societies. By studying and building upon the accomplishments of these ancient cultures, we can better appreciate the rich tapestry of human ingenuity and the enduring legacy of scientific inquiry across diverse civilizations throughout history.

Early Greek Science and Philosophy

Early Greek Science and Philosophy played a crucial role in laying the foundation for the development of scientific thought and inquiry. This period, marked by intellectual curiosity and a quest for understanding the natural world, saw the emergence of key figures such as Thales, Pythagoras, and Aristotle, whose contributions have had a lasting impact on various fields of study.

Thales, known as one of the Seven Sages of Greece, is often considered the first philosopher in Western tradition. He is credited with introducing the concept of seeking natural explanations for phenomena rather than attributing them to supernatural forces. Thales made significant contributions to geometry, particularly in the realm of mathematics. His exploration of geometric principles paved the way for the development of mathematical reasoning and the understanding of shapes and proportions in the physical world. Additionally, Thales is known for his work in astronomy, where he made predictions about celestial events based on empirical observations rather than mythological beliefs.

Pythagoras, another prominent figure in early Greek science and philosophy, is renowned for his contributions to mathematics and music theory. The Pythagorean theorem, which states that the square of the hypotenuse of a right-angled triangle is equal to the sum of the squares of the other two sides, is one of his most enduring mathematical discoveries. Pythagoras also delved into the study of harmonics and the relationship between numerical ratios and musical intervals, laying the groundwork for the mathematical understanding of music and sound.

Aristotle, often regarded as one of the greatest thinkers in history, made significant contributions across multiple disciplines, including biology, physics, and ethics. In biology, Aristotle's systematic observations and classifications of living organisms laid the groundwork for the field of natural history. His work on animal anatomy and behavior influenced the study of zoology for centuries to come. In physics, Aristotle proposed a comprehensive system of understanding the natural world by categorizing motion, matter, and causation. His ideas on the elements and the structure of the universe shaped scientific thought for generations. Furthermore, Aristotle's ethical philosophy, centered on the concept of virtue and the pursuit of eudaimonia (human flourishing), continues to be a foundational principle in moral philosophy.

Overall, the contributions of Thales, Pythagoras, and Aristotle in early Greek science and philosophy exemplify the spirit of inquiry, rational thinking, and empirical observation that are fundamental to the scientific method. Their work not only advanced human understanding of the natural world but also laid the groundwork for future scientific developments in mathematics, astronomy, biology, physics, and ethics. The legacy of these ancient Greek thinkers continues to inspire and influence scientific inquiry and philosophical discourse to this day.

Chapter 2

Classical Science

Advancements in Hellenistic Science

Advancements in Hellenistic Science during the Classical period marked a significant era of scientific progress and innovation, building upon the foundational knowledge laid out by earlier civilizations. In this chapter, we delve into the remarkable contributions of three prominent figures – Euclid, Archimedes, and Ptolemy – who played pivotal roles in shaping the fields of geometry, mechanics, hydrostatics, astronomy, and geography.

Euclid, known as the "Father of Geometry," revolutionized the study of mathematics with his seminal work, "Elements." This comprehensive treatise encompassed various geometric principles and theorems, providing a systematic approach to the understanding of shapes, angles, and spatial relationships. Euclid's deductive reasoning and logical proofs laid the groundwork for the development of geometry as a formal discipline, influencing mathematical thought for centuries to come.

Archimedes, a brilliant mathematician, physicist, and inventor, made significant advancements in the fields of mechanics and hydrostatics. His principle of buoyancy, known as Archimedes' principle, revolutionized the understanding of fluid mechanics and the behavior of objects immersed in liquids. Additionally, Archimedes formulated fundamental concepts in levers, pulleys, and the calculation of areas and volumes, showcasing his prowess in both theoretical and applied mathematics.

Ptolemy, an astronomer and mathematician, made enduring contributions to the fields of astronomy and geography. His astronomical work, "Almagest," presented a geocentric model of the universe that dominated Western thought for over a millennium. Ptolemy's detailed observations of celestial bodies, combined with his mathematical calculations, led to the development of intricate models of planetary motion and stellar positions, laying the foundation for future astronomical studies.

Furthermore, Ptolemy's geographical treatise, "Geography," provided a comprehensive overview of the known world at that time, mapping out regions, cities, and landmarks with remarkable accuracy. His use of latitude and longitude coordinates, along with his systematic approach to cartography, advanced the field of geography and influenced navigational practices for centuries to come.

The collective work of Euclid, Archimedes, and Ptolemy exemplifies the intellectual vibrancy and scientific ingenuity of the Hellenistic period. Their contributions not only expanded the frontiers of knowledge in mathematics, physics, and astronomy but also paved the way for future generations of scientists and scholars to build upon their groundbreaking discoveries.

In conclusion, the advancements in Hellenistic science, as exemplified by the pioneering work of Euclid, Archimedes, and Ptolemy, represent a golden age of scientific inquiry and innovation. Their enduring legacies continue to inspire and inform contemporary scientific endeavors, underscoring the timeless relevance of their contributions to the evolution of human knowledge and understanding.

Roman Contributions to Science and Technology

The Romans were renowned for their engineering prowess, which played a vital role in shaping the infrastructure of their vast empire. One of the most iconic Roman innovations was the aqueduct system. These monumental structures were designed to transport water from distant sources to urban centers, ensuring a stable water supply for public baths, fountains, and private residences. The engineering marvel of aqueducts showcased the Romans' expertise in hydraulics, surveying, and construction.

In addition to aqueducts, Roman road networks were another remarkable achievement that facilitated communication, trade, and military operations across the empire. The Romans constructed an extensive network of well-engineered roads, such as the famous Appian Way, which connected major cities and provinces. These roads were paved with durable materials like gravel, sand, and stone, incorporating sophisticated drainage systems to withstand heavy traffic and adverse weather conditions.

Roman medical practices also made significant contributions to the field of healthcare. Roman physicians borrowed knowledge from Greek and Egyptian medicine and developed their own medical techniques and treatments. They established public hospitals, known as valetudinaria, where patients could receive medical care, surgery, and rehabilitation. Roman doctors advanced the understanding of anatomy through dissections and surgical procedures, paving the way for future medical advancements.

Natural history flourished in ancient Rome, with notable figures like Pliny the Elder making significant contributions to the field. Pliny's encyclopedic work, "Natural History," compiled a vast array of knowledge on topics ranging from botany and zoology to geology and meteorology. This comprehensive compilation served as a valuable resource for scholars and researchers interested in the natural world, providing insights into the diversity and complexity of the environment.

Overall, Roman contributions to science and technology were instrumental in shaping the development of Western civilization. Their engineering feats, such as aqueducts and roads, not only improved the quality of life for Roman citizens but also influenced future generations in the fields of architecture and civil engineering. The advancements in medical practices and natural history reflected the Romans' curiosity and dedication to understanding the world around them. By embracing innovation and practicality, the Romans left a lasting legacy that continues to inspire and inform scientific endeavors to this day.

The Decline of Classical Science and the Preservation of Knowledge

The decline of classical science marked a significant shift in the intellectual landscape of the Western world following the fall of the Western Roman Empire. As the empire crumbled under the weight of internal strife, external invasions, and economic challenges, the once-thriving centers of learning and scientific inquiry faced disruptions and disintegration. However, amidst this decline, the preservation of classical knowledge emerged as a crucial endeavor undertaken by various cultural and religious groups, including Byzantine, Islamic, and monastic scholars.

Following the collapse of the Western Roman Empire in the 5th century CE, the preservation of classical knowledge became a priority for the Byzantine Empire, which rose as the successor to the Eastern Roman Empire. Byzantine scholars played a pivotal role in safeguarding and transmitting ancient Greek and Roman texts on diverse subjects ranging from philosophy and mathematics to medicine and astronomy. Libraries and centers of learning, such as the renowned Library of Constantinople, served as repositories of this inherited knowledge, ensuring its survival amidst the tumultuous political and social climate of the time.

Simultaneously, the Islamic world experienced a period of intellectual flourishing known as the Islamic Golden Age, during which Islamic scholars made significant contributions to the preservation and advancement of scientific knowledge. The translation movement, centered around institutions like the House of Wisdom in Baghdad, facilitated the translation of Greek, Persian, and Indian texts into Arabic, thereby preserving and disseminating classical wisdom to a wider audience. Scholars like Al-Khwarizmi, Ibn Sina, and Alhazen made groundbreaking contributions in fields such as mathematics, medicine, and optics, enriching the scientific heritage of humanity.

In addition to the Byzantine and Islamic realms, monastic scholars in medieval Europe played a crucial role in the preservation of classical knowledge during the tumultuous period following the fall of the Western Roman Empire. Monasteries served as centers of learning and scriptoria where monks meticulously copied and preserved ancient manuscripts, including works of classical authors like Aristotle, Plato, and Euclid. Monastic libraries became repositories of knowledge, ensuring that ancient texts were not lost to the ravages of time and political upheaval.

The preservation of classical knowledge by Byzantine, Islamic, and monastic scholars not only safeguarded the intellectual legacy of antiquity but also laid the foundation for the revival of learning and scholarship in later centuries. The transmission of ancient scientific and philosophical texts across cultural and geographical boundaries facilitated the cross-fertilization of ideas and the emergence of new intellectual movements that would shape the course of scientific inquiry in the centuries to come.

In conclusion, the decline of classical science following the fall of the Western Roman Empire was mitigated by the dedicated efforts of Byzantine, Islamic, and monastic scholars to preserve and transmit classical knowledge to future generations. Their commitment to safeguarding the intellectual heritage of antiquity played a crucial role in shaping the trajectory of scientific thought and inquiry, ensuring that the wisdom of the past continued to inspire and inform the scientific endeavors of the present and the future.

Chapter 3

Science in the Islamic Golden Age

The Translation Movement and the House of Wisdom in Baghdad

The translation movement and the establishment of the House of Wisdom in Baghdad during the Islamic Golden Age marked a significant period in the history of science and knowledge exchange. This chapter delves into the transformative impact of translating Greek and Persian texts into Arabic and the pivotal role played by the House of Wisdom in facilitating the dissemination of scientific knowledge.

The Translation Movement:
During the Islamic Golden Age, from the 8th to the 14th centuries, the translation movement played a crucial role in bridging the gap between different cultures and preserving the scientific heritage of antiquity. Scholars in the Islamic world recognized the value of ancient Greek and Persian texts in fields such as philosophy, mathematics, astronomy, medicine, and optics. These texts were translated into Arabic, serving as a foundation for further advancements in scientific inquiry.

The House of Wisdom:
One of the most prominent institutions that emerged during this period was the House of Wisdom in Baghdad, established in the 9th century under the Abbasid Caliphate. The House of Wisdom

served as a center for intellectual pursuits, where scholars, translators, and scientists from diverse backgrounds gathered to study, discuss, and translate works from various civilizations.

Translation Activities:
The scholars at the House of Wisdom undertook the monumental task of translating a vast array of texts from Greek, Persian, Indian, and other languages into Arabic. These translations encompassed works by renowned thinkers such as Aristotle, Plato, Euclid, Ptolemy, Hippocrates, and many others. Through these efforts, Arabic became a lingua franca for scientific and philosophical discourse, facilitating the exchange of ideas across different cultures.

Impact on Scientific Advancements:
The translations carried out at the House of Wisdom played a pivotal role in shaping the intellectual landscape of the Islamic world and beyond. They laid the groundwork for significant advancements in various fields, including mathematics, astronomy, medicine, and optics. Scholars like Al-Khwarizmi, Ibn Sina, and Alhazen built upon the translated works to make groundbreaking contributions that influenced scientific thought for centuries to come.

Legacy and Influence:
The legacy of the translation movement and the House of Wisdom extended far beyond the Islamic Golden Age, contributing to the transmission of knowledge to medieval Europe and shaping the development of Western science. The translations preserved and expanded upon the works of ancient scholars, fostering a spirit of curiosity and inquiry that underpinned scientific progress in subsequent centuries.

In conclusion, the translation movement and the establishment of the House of Wisdom in Baghdad exemplify the transformative power of cross-cultural exchange and intellectual collaboration. By translating and disseminating ancient scientific texts, scholars at the House of Wisdom played a vital role in preserving and advancing the legacy of scientific knowledge, laying the foundation for the flourishing of science and scholarship in the Islamic world and beyond.

Key Figures in the Islamic Golden Age

During the Islamic Golden Age, a period of significant cultural, economic, and scientific flourishing in the Islamic world from the 8th to the 14th century, several key figures made groundbreaking contributions to various fields of knowledge. Among these luminaries were Al-Khwarizmi, Ibn Sina, and Alhazen, whose work not only advanced their respective fields but also laid the foundation for future scientific progress.

Al-Khwarizmi, often referred to as the "father of algebra," was a Persian mathematician, astronomer, and geographer who lived during the 9th century. His most enduring legacy lies in his foundational work on algebra, where he introduced systematic methods for solving linear and quadratic equations. Al-Khwarizmi's treatise on algebra, known as "Kitab al-Jabr wal-Muqabala," not only standardized algebraic notation and terminology but also introduced the concept of algorithms, a term derived from his name. His contributions to mathematics were instrumental in the development of algebra as a distinct branch of mathematics and had a profound influence on subsequent mathematicians in both the Islamic and Western worlds.

Ibn Sina, also known as Avicenna, was a Persian polymath who lived in the 11th century and made significant contributions to medicine, philosophy, and various other fields. His most famous work, "The Canon of Medicine," became a standard medical textbook in Europe and the Islamic world for over six centuries. In this comprehensive medical encyclopedia, Ibn Sina synthesized the medical knowledge of the time and introduced numerous innovations, including the distinction between infectious and contagious diseases and the concept of clinical trials. Beyond medicine, Ibn Sina's philosophical works, particularly his metaphysical and epistemological writings, had a lasting impact on Islamic and Western philosophy, earning him a prominent place in the history of thought.

Alhazen, also known as Ibn al-Haytham, was an Arab polymath who lived in the 10th and 11th centuries and is often regarded as the "father of modern optics." His most famous work, "Kitab al-Manazir" or "Book of Optics," revolutionized the understanding of light, vision, and the nature of optics. Alhazen's experimental approach to optics, which emphasized observation, experimentation, and empirical verification, laid the foundation for the scientific method in optics and influenced later scientific thinkers, including European luminaries like Roger Bacon and Johannes Kepler. His work on the anatomy of the eye, the nature of light, and the principles of visual perception marked a significant departure from the Greek theories of vision and established a new paradigm for the study of optics.

In conclusion, the contributions of Al-Khwarizmi, Ibn Sina, and Alhazen exemplify the rich intellectual legacy of the Islamic Golden Age. These key figures not only advanced knowledge in their respective fields of mathematics, medicine, and optics but also played a crucial role in shaping the development of scientific thought and methodology. By fostering a spirit of inquiry, innovation, and empirical investigation, they laid the groundwork for the scientific advancements that would follow in the centuries to come.

Contributions in Mathematics, Astronomy, Medicine, and Optics

During the Islamic Golden Age, significant advancements were made in various fields including mathematics, astronomy, medicine, and optics. These contributions not only built upon the knowledge of ancient civilizations but also laid the foundation for future scientific progress.

In mathematics, one of the most notable figures was Al-Khwarizmi, who is often referred to as the "father of algebra." He was instrumental in introducing systematic methods for solving linear and quadratic equations, laying down the groundwork for algebra as a distinct mathematical discipline. Al-Khwarizmi's work also led to the development of algorithms, which are essential in modern computer science and cryptography.

The Islamic scholars also made significant strides in astronomy. The development of the astrolabe, a sophisticated instrument used for measuring the positions of celestial objects and for navigation, was a major achievement. This device revolutionized the study of astronomy and greatly enhanced navigational accuracy for sailors and astronomers alike.

In the field of medicine, Islamic scholars compiled vast encyclopedias that synthesized medical knowledge from ancient Greek, Persian, and Indian sources. One of the most famous works was the Canon of Medicine by Ibn Sina (Avicenna), which became a standard medical textbook in Europe for centuries. These medical encyclopedias not only preserved ancient medical knowledge but also added new insights and treatments, contributing to the advancement of medical science.

The Islamic Golden Age also saw significant progress in optics, with scholars like Alhazen making crucial contributions to the understanding of light and vision. Alhazen's groundbreaking work on optics laid the foundation for the scientific method of experimentation and observation. His studies on the behavior of light and the anatomy of the eye paved the way for advancements in optics that would later influence developments in fields such as photography and ophthalmology.

Overall, the contributions in mathematics, astronomy, medicine, and optics during the Islamic Golden Age were instrumental in shaping the course of scientific progress. These advancements not only enriched the existing knowledge base but also inspired future generations of scientists and scholars to further explore the mysteries of the universe. The legacy of these scholars continues to resonate in modern science, highlighting the enduring impact of the Islamic Golden Age on the development of human knowledge and understanding.

Chapter 4

Medieval European Science

The Carolingian Renaissance and the Revival of Learning

The Carolingian Renaissance, a period of intellectual and cultural revival in Europe during the reign of Charlemagne in the late 8th and early 9th centuries, marked a significant turning point in the history of science and learning. Charlemagne, also known as Charles the Great, was a Frankish king who became the first Holy Roman Emperor in 800 AD. His efforts to promote education and scholarship played a crucial role in the preservation and transmission of knowledge from classical antiquity to the medieval period.

One of Charlemagne's key initiatives was the establishment of a palace school at his court in Aachen, where scholars from across Europe were invited to study and teach a wide range of subjects, including grammar, rhetoric, mathematics, astronomy, and theology. This emphasis on education laid the foundation for the Carolingian Renaissance, which saw a revival of interest in classical texts, the promotion of literacy, and the development of a standardized script known as Carolingian minuscule.

Under Charlemagne's patronage, a group of scholars known as the "Palace School" or the "Circle of Aachen" worked to translate and preserve ancient manuscripts, particularly those of Latin and Greek authors. These efforts led to the creation of new copies of classical works, many of which would have been lost without Charlemagne's support for scholarship and intellectual pursuits.

Furthermore, Charlemagne's promotion of learning extended beyond his court to the establishment of monastic and cathedral schools throughout the Carolingian Empire. These schools played a crucial role in the dissemination of knowledge, with monks and clergy serving as both educators and scribes, copying and preserving ancient texts for future generations.

The Carolingian Renaissance also saw the development of a new educational curriculum that emphasized the liberal arts, including the trivium (grammar, rhetoric, logic) and the quadrivium (arithmetic, geometry, music, astronomy). This holistic approach to education aimed to cultivate well-rounded individuals who were proficient in both secular and religious knowledge.

In addition to his educational reforms, Charlemagne's support for learning was also evident in his patronage of prominent scholars and intellectuals, such as Alcuin of York, an English scholar who served as Charlemagne's chief advisor on educational matters. Alcuin played a key role in shaping the curriculum of the palace school and promoting the study of classical texts.

Overall, the Carolingian Renaissance under Charlemagne's leadership marked a period of intellectual renewal and cultural revitalization in Europe. By fostering a climate of learning and scholarship, Charlemagne laid the groundwork for the preservation and transmission of classical knowledge, setting the stage for future advancements in science, philosophy, and the arts in the medieval period and beyond.

Scholasticism and the Integration of Greek and Islamic Science

During the medieval period in Europe, a movement known as Scholasticism emerged as a way to reconcile Christian theology with the teachings of ancient Greek and Islamic scholars. This intellectual movement played a crucial role in shaping the landscape of scientific inquiry and education in medieval universities.

One of the key figures in Scholasticism was Thomas Aquinas, a Dominican friar and theologian known for his synthesis of Christian doctrine with Aristotelian philosophy. Aquinas believed that reason and faith could coexist harmoniously, and he sought to integrate the teachings of Aristotle into Christian theology. His influential work, "Summa Theologica," provided a framework for discussing theological and philosophical questions using logical reasoning and empirical observation. Aquinas's emphasis on reason and logic paved the way for a more systematic approach to knowledge that would influence generations of scholars.

Another significant figure in the integration of Greek and Islamic science was Roger Bacon, an English Franciscan friar and philosopher. Bacon was a proponent of empirical methods and believed that knowledge should be acquired through direct observation and experimentation. He emphasized the importance of empirical evidence in the pursuit of scientific truth, a departure from the prevailing reliance on authority and tradition in medieval scholarship. Bacon's insistence on the importance of observation laid the groundwork for the rise of experimental science and the scientific method in later centuries.

The establishment of medieval universities also played a crucial role in facilitating the integration of Greek and Islamic science into European intellectual discourse. These institutions, such as the University of Paris and the University of Oxford, became centers of learning where scholars from different cultural and religious backgrounds could exchange ideas and knowledge. The curriculum at medieval universities included a wide range of subjects, including natural philosophy, astronomy, mathematics, and medicine, drawing on the rich traditions of Greek, Islamic, and Christian scholarship.

Scholasticism and the integration of Greek and Islamic science marked a significant shift in medieval thought, paving the way for the development of modern scientific inquiry. By emphasizing the importance of reason, observation, and empirical evidence, scholars like Thomas Aquinas and Roger Bacon laid the foundation for a more systematic and evidence-based approach to understanding the natural world. Their efforts to reconcile diverse intellectual traditions helped bridge the gap between faith and reason, setting the stage for the scientific advancements of the Renaissance and the Enlightenment.

Developments in Natural Philosophy and Early Universities

During the medieval period, the development of natural philosophy and the establishment of early universities played a crucial role in fostering intellectual growth and scientific inquiry. Early universities served as centers of learning where scholars from diverse backgrounds came together to exchange ideas, study ancient texts, and engage in intellectual debates. These institutions laid the foundation for the growth of scientific knowledge and the advancement of natural philosophy.

One of the key aspects of natural philosophy during this time was the integration of knowledge from various sources, including Greek, Islamic, and Christian traditions. Scholars in medieval universities studied works by ancient philosophers such as Aristotle, Ptolemy, and Euclid, as well as texts translated from Arabic sources. This cross-cultural exchange of ideas and knowledge facilitated the synthesis of different scientific and philosophical traditions, leading to new insights and discoveries.

The curriculum in early universities focused on the liberal arts, which included subjects like arithmetic, geometry, music, and astronomy. These disciplines were considered essential for cultivating a well-rounded education and developing critical thinking skills. Students were encouraged to engage in debates, discussions, and disputation, which helped sharpen their intellectual abilities and deepen their understanding of natural phenomena.

One of the significant contributions of early universities was the development of scholasticism, a philosophical and theological system that sought to reconcile faith with reason. Scholars like Thomas Aquinas played a key role in integrating Aristotelian philosophy with Christian theology, creating a framework for understanding the natural world through a combination of observation, reason, and revelation.

The establishment of medieval universities also provided a supportive environment for scientific inquiry and experimentation. Scholars conducted experiments, made observations, and documented their findings, laying the groundwork for the empirical approach to scientific investigation that would later become central to the scientific method.

Moreover, the growth of universities during this period led to the establishment of scientific communities and networks of scholars who shared a common interest in advancing knowledge and understanding of the natural world. These communities provided a platform for collaboration, communication, and the dissemination of scientific ideas, contributing to the rapid exchange of information and the acceleration of scientific progress.

In conclusion, the developments in natural philosophy and the establishment of early universities during the medieval period played a pivotal role in shaping the course of scientific inquiry and intellectual progress. These institutions provided a fertile ground for the synthesis of diverse intellectual traditions, the cultivation of critical thinking skills, and the promotion of empirical investigation. The legacy of early universities continues to influence the practice of science and the pursuit of knowledge to this day.

Chapter 5

The Renaissance and the Scientific Revolution

The Rediscovery of Classical Texts and the Rise of Humanism

The Renaissance period marked a significant shift in intellectual and cultural attitudes in Europe, leading to the rediscovery of classical texts and the rise of humanism. This era, spanning from the 14th to the 17th century, was characterized by a renewed interest in the achievements of ancient civilizations, particularly those of Greece and Rome. The impact of the Renaissance on the revival of classical learning and the promotion of humanist ideals had a profound influence on the development of science and scientific thought.

One of the key aspects of the Renaissance was the rediscovery of classical texts that had been preserved and translated by scholars during the Islamic Golden Age. The availability of these texts, which covered a wide range of subjects including philosophy, mathematics, astronomy, and medicine, provided European scholars with access to a wealth of knowledge that had been largely lost or forgotten during the Middle Ages. This rediscovery of ancient works allowed for a reexamination of the natural world based on empirical observation and rational inquiry, laying the foundation for the scientific revolution that would follow.

The humanist movement of the Renaissance emphasized the importance of individual human potential and the pursuit of knowledge for its own sake. Humanist scholars sought to emulate the intellectual achievements of the ancient Greeks and Romans, viewing them as models of wisdom and learning. Humanism promoted a more secular and rational approach to understanding the world, encouraging scholars to rely on observation and reason rather than tradition or authority.

The impact of humanism on science was profound, as it encouraged a shift away from the reliance on religious dogma and superstition that had dominated medieval thought. Humanist scholars such as Leonardo da Vinci and Galileo Galilei championed the importance of direct observation and experimentation in the pursuit of knowledge. Their work laid the groundwork for the development of the scientific method, a systematic approach to inquiry that would revolutionize the study of the natural world.

The emphasis on empirical observation and critical thinking promoted by humanism paved the way for significant advancements in fields such as astronomy, physics, and biology. Scientists like Nicolaus Copernicus, who proposed a heliocentric model of the universe, and Johannes Kepler, who formulated laws of planetary motion, built upon the humanist ideals of reason and observation to challenge established beliefs and expand the boundaries of scientific knowledge.

In conclusion, the rediscovery of classical texts and the rise of humanism during the Renaissance had a transformative impact on the development of science. By promoting the importance of empirical observation, rational inquiry, and critical thinking, humanist scholars laid the foundation for the scientific revolution and the modern scientific method. The revival of classical learning and the humanist emphasis on individual potential and intellectual curiosity created a fertile intellectual environment that fostered innovation and discovery, shaping the course of scientific inquiry for centuries to come.

Key Figures of the Scientific Revolution

The Scientific Revolution, a period of profound intellectual transformation in the 16th and 17th centuries, was marked by groundbreaking advancements in scientific thought and methodology. Key figures of this era played pivotal roles in challenging traditional beliefs, revolutionizing our understanding of the natural world, and laying the foundation for modern science. In this section, we will delve into the significant contributions of four key figures of the Scientific Revolution: Copernicus, Galileo, Kepler, and Newton.

Nicolaus Copernicus, a Polish mathematician and astronomer, is renowned for his heliocentric model of the universe. In his seminal work "De Revolutionibus Orbium Coelestium" (On the Revolutions of the Celestial Spheres), Copernicus proposed that the Earth and other planets revolve around the Sun, contradicting the geocentric model that placed Earth at the center of the universe. This heliocentric theory laid the groundwork for modern astronomy and challenged the prevailing Ptolemaic system, leading to a paradigm shift in cosmological understanding.

Galileo Galilei, an Italian physicist, mathematician, and astronomer, made significant contributions to the fields of telescopic astronomy and mechanics. Through his observations with the newly invented telescope, Galileo discovered the moons of Jupiter, observed sunspots, and confirmed the phases of Venus, providing empirical evidence in support of the Copernican heliocentric model. His experiments on motion and gravity laid the groundwork for the development of classical mechanics and influenced the work of later scientists, including Isaac Newton.

Johannes Kepler, a German mathematician and astronomer, is renowned for his laws of planetary motion. Kepler's three laws, derived from his meticulous observations of the motion of Mars and other planets, revolutionized our understanding of celestial mechanics. Kepler's laws provided a mathematical framework for describing the orbits of planets around the Sun, replacing the earlier geocentric and heliocentric models with a more accurate and elegant system based on elliptical orbits and equal areas swept out in equal times.

Sir Isaac Newton, an English physicist and mathematician, is considered one of the greatest scientists in history. Newton's work on the laws of motion and universal gravitation laid the foundation for classical physics and transformed our understanding of the physical universe. In his seminal work "Philosophiæ Naturalis Principia Mathematica" (Mathematical Principles of Natural Philosophy), Newton formulated his three laws of motion and the law of universal gravitation, providing a unified explanation for the motion of objects on Earth and in the heavens. Newton's laws of motion and gravity revolutionized physics and set the stage for the development of modern science.

In conclusion, the key figures of the Scientific Revolution, including Copernicus, Galileo, Kepler, and Newton, played instrumental roles in reshaping our understanding of the cosmos and laying the groundwork for modern science. Their groundbreaking work in astronomy, mechanics, and mathematics not only challenged prevailing beliefs but also set the stage for centuries of scientific progress and discovery. The legacy of these visionary thinkers continues to inspire and inform scientific inquiry to this day.

The Development of the Scientific Method and Experimental Science

The scientific method is a systematic approach to inquiry that has revolutionized the way we understand the natural world. It involves a structured process of observation, hypothesis formation, experimentation, and analysis to test and refine our understanding of phenomena. The development of the scientific method is attributed to key figures such as Francis Bacon and René Descartes, who played pivotal roles in shaping the foundations of modern science.

Francis Bacon, an English philosopher, statesman, and scientist, is often credited with formalizing the scientific method in his seminal work, Novum Organum (1620). Bacon emphasized the importance of empirical observation and inductive reasoning in the pursuit of knowledge. He advocated for a methodical approach to experimentation, where observations are systematically collected and analyzed to derive general principles. Bacon's emphasis on the systematic collection of data and the importance of experimentation laid the groundwork for modern scientific inquiry.

René Descartes, a French philosopher and mathematician, also made significant contributions to the development of the scientific method. In his work Discourse on the Method (1637), Descartes outlined a deductive approach to knowledge, famously encapsulated in his dictum "cogito, ergo sum" (I think, therefore I am). Descartes emphasized the importance of doubt and skepticism in arriving at certain truths, advocating for a method that starts from self-evident axioms and proceeds through logical reasoning to arrive at conclusions. Descartes's emphasis on deductive reasoning and the importance of clear and distinct ideas influenced the rationalistic tradition in science.

The scientific method, as articulated by Bacon and Descartes, revolutionized scientific inquiry by providing a structured framework for investigating the natural world. It emphasized the importance of systematic observation, experimentation, and logical reasoning in the pursuit of knowledge. The rise of experimental science marked a departure from traditional modes of inquiry based on authority and received wisdom, paving the way for a new era of empirical investigation and discovery.

Experimental science involves the design and conduct of controlled experiments to test hypotheses and theories. By manipulating variables and measuring outcomes, scientists can systematically investigate the causal relationships between phenomena. Experimental science allows for the rigorous testing of hypotheses, leading to the accumulation of empirical evidence and the refinement of scientific theories.

The formulation of the scientific method by Bacon and Descartes laid the groundwork for the development of modern experimental science. Their emphasis on empirical observation, systematic experimentation, and logical reasoning continues to shape the practice of science today. The scientific method remains a cornerstone of scientific inquiry, guiding researchers in their quest to uncover the mysteries of the natural world and advance human knowledge.

Chapter 6

The Age of Enlightenment

The Role of Science in Enlightenment Thought

The Enlightenment period, also known as the Age of Reason, was a transformative era in the history of science and philosophy. During this time, thinkers and scholars sought to apply reason, logic, and empirical evidence to understand the natural world and human society. The influence of key figures such as René Descartes, Gottfried Wilhelm Leibniz, and John Locke played a crucial role in shaping Enlightenment thought and advancing scientific inquiry.

René Descartes, a French philosopher and mathematician, is often referred to as the "father of modern philosophy" due to his emphasis on the use of reason and skepticism in the pursuit of knowledge. Descartes' famous statement, "Cogito, ergo sum" (I think, therefore I am), epitomizes his belief in the power of human reason to discern truth. In his work, Descartes sought to establish a foundation of knowledge based on clear and distinct ideas, laying the groundwork for the scientific method and the rationalist tradition in philosophy.

Gottfried Wilhelm Leibniz, a German polymath, made significant contributions to mathematics, philosophy, and logic during the Enlightenment period. Leibniz is best known for his development of calculus independently of Isaac Newton, as well as his work on metaphysics and the philosophy of mind. His concept of the "monad," a metaphysical entity that represents the fundamental building block of the universe, influenced later philosophical and scientific thought.

John Locke, an English philosopher and physician, is renowned for his empiricist theory of knowledge and his ideas on political philosophy. Locke argued that all knowledge is derived from sensory experience, challenging traditional notions of innate ideas. His work laid the foundation for modern empiricism and the scientific method, emphasizing the importance of observation, experimentation, and evidence in the pursuit of knowledge.

The ideas of Descartes, Leibniz, and Locke had a profound impact on Enlightenment thinking, shaping the intellectual landscape of the period. Their emphasis on reason, empiricism, and the importance of individual inquiry laid the groundwork for advancements in various scientific disciplines, including physics, chemistry, biology, and medicine.

Enlightenment thinkers sought to challenge traditional authority, superstition, and dogma through the application of reason and critical thinking. This spirit of inquiry and skepticism paved the way for scientific progress and the development of new theories and discoveries that revolutionized our understanding of the natural world.

In conclusion, the role of science in Enlightenment thought was characterized by a commitment to rational inquiry, empirical evidence, and the pursuit of knowledge through observation and experimentation. Descartes, Leibniz, and Locke were instrumental in shaping the intellectual climate of the Enlightenment, laying the foundation for modern science and the scientific method. Their influence continues to be felt in contemporary scientific research and scholarship, highlighting the enduring legacy of Enlightenment ideals in the pursuit of truth and understanding.

Advancements in Chemistry, Biology, and Physics

Advancements in Chemistry, Biology, and Physics in the history of science have been pivotal in shaping our understanding of the natural world and driving technological progress. This section will delve into the significant contributions of Robert Boyle, Antoine Lavoisier, and Carl Linnaeus to their respective fields, highlighting their groundbreaking work and lasting impact on scientific thought.

Robert Boyle, known as the "Father of Modern Chemistry," made significant strides in the field of chemistry during the 17th century. Boyle's most notable contribution was his formulation of Boyle's Law, which describes the inverse relationship between the pressure and volume of a gas at constant temperature. This fundamental principle laid the groundwork for the development of the gas laws and provided a quantitative basis for understanding the behavior of gases. Boyle's experiments and writings also helped to establish chemistry as a distinct scientific discipline, separate from alchemy.

Antoine Lavoisier, often referred to as the "Father of Modern Chemistry," revolutionized the field of chemistry in the late 18th century. Lavoisier is best known for his meticulous experiments on combustion and his identification of oxygen as a key element in the process. He also introduced the concept of the conservation of mass, stating that matter is neither created nor destroyed in chemical reactions but merely rearranged. Lavoisier's systematic approach to studying chemical reactions and his development of a nomenclature system for naming chemical substances laid the foundation for modern chemistry and helped to establish it as a quantitative science.

Carl Linnaeus, a Swedish botanist and zoologist, made significant contributions to the field of biology with his development of the binomial nomenclature system for classifying living organisms. Linnaeus's system of naming species based on genus and species helped to standardize the classification of plants and animals and provided a universal language for biologists to communicate. His work laid the groundwork for modern taxonomy and systematics, establishing a hierarchical framework for organizing the diversity of life on Earth.

In addition to their individual contributions, the work of Boyle, Lavoisier, and Linnaeus collectively advanced our understanding of the natural world and laid the foundation for further discoveries in chemistry, biology, and physics. Their emphasis on empirical observation, systematic experimentation, and logical reasoning exemplifies the scientific method and the spirit of inquiry that continues to drive scientific progress to this day.

Overall, the advancements made by Boyle, Lavoisier, and Linnaeus in the fields of chemistry, biology, and physics have had a profound impact on scientific thought and have paved the way for modern scientific inquiry. Their work exemplifies the power of curiosity, innovation, and collaboration in advancing human knowledge and understanding of the world around us.

The Establishment of Scientific Societies and Academies

The establishment of scientific societies and academies played a crucial role in shaping the landscape of scientific inquiry and collaboration during various periods of history. Two prominent examples of such institutions are the Royal Society in England and the Académie des Sciences in France. These organizations were founded with the aim of promoting scientific research, communication, and collaboration among scholars and scientists.

The Royal Society, established in London in 1660, holds the distinction of being one of the oldest scientific academies in the world. It was founded by a group of natural philosophers, including Robert Boyle and Robert Hooke, with the purpose of fostering scientific experimentation and knowledge sharing. The Royal Society played a key role in the development of experimental science and the scientific method. Members of the society conducted experiments, presented their findings to their peers, and engaged in lively discussions and debates on various scientific topics.

The Royal Society also played a significant role in the publication of scientific research through its journal, "Philosophical Transactions." This journal provided a platform for scientists to disseminate their discoveries and findings to a wider audience, thus contributing to the advancement of scientific knowledge. The society's motto, "Nullius in verba" (Latin for "take nobody's word for it"), reflects its commitment to empirical evidence and the importance of independent verification in scientific inquiry.

Similarly, the Académie des Sciences, founded in Paris in 1666, aimed to promote scientific research and education in France. The academy brought together leading scientists, mathematicians, and philosophers to discuss and collaborate on various scientific endeavors. Members of the academy worked on a wide range of scientific disciplines, including mathematics, physics, astronomy, and chemistry.

The Académie des Sciences played a pivotal role in advancing scientific knowledge in France and beyond. Its members made significant contributions to fields such as mechanics, optics, and biology. The academy also published scientific papers and journals to share the latest research findings with the scientific community.

Both the Royal Society and the Académie des Sciences served as important hubs for scientific communication and collaboration. These institutions provided a platform for scientists to exchange ideas, share research findings, and engage in intellectual debates. By fostering a culture of open inquiry and rigorous scientific investigation, these societies played a key role in driving scientific progress and innovation during their respective time periods.

In conclusion, the establishment of scientific societies and academies such as the Royal Society and the Académie des Sciences played a vital role in promoting scientific communication, collaboration, and knowledge sharing. These institutions provided a platform for scientists to conduct experiments, present their research, and engage in intellectual discourse, ultimately contributing to the advancement of scientific knowledge and the development of modern science.

Chapter 7

The Industrial Revolution and the Rise of Modern Science

The Impact of Industrialization on Scientific Research and Technology

The Industrial Revolution, a period of significant economic and technological change that began in the late 18th century, had a profound impact on scientific research and technology. This transformative era marked a shift from agrarian and handicraft-based economies to industrialized societies driven by machinery, mass production, and improved transportation systems. The impact of industrialization on scientific advancements in engineering, manufacturing, and transportation was revolutionary and laid the foundation for the modern world we live in today.

Engineering Advancements:

One of the key impacts of industrialization on scientific research was the rapid progress in engineering. The demand for more efficient machinery and infrastructure to support growing industries led to innovations in various engineering fields. Engineers developed new techniques and materials to construct bridges, railways, factories, and other structures that could withstand the demands of industrial production. The development of steam-powered engines, such as James Watt's improved steam engine, revolutionized manufacturing processes and transportation systems, leading to increased productivity and economic growth.

Manufacturing Innovations:
Industrialization also drove advancements in manufacturing processes and techniques. The introduction of mechanized production methods, including the use of water and steam power, enabled the mass production of goods on a scale never seen before. Innovations in textile manufacturing, such as the spinning jenny and power loom, transformed the textile industry and paved the way for the factory system. The standardization of parts and the implementation of assembly line production methods streamlined manufacturing processes and increased efficiency and output.

Transportation Revolution:
The Industrial Revolution had a profound impact on transportation systems, leading to the development of faster and more reliable modes of travel. The construction of canals, roads, and railways facilitated the movement of goods and people across vast distances, connecting markets and fostering trade. The invention of the steam locomotive by George Stephenson and the expansion of railway networks revolutionized transportation, making travel faster, cheaper, and more accessible. The steamship also transformed maritime transportation, enabling faster and more efficient oceanic travel.

Overall, the Industrial Revolution spurred advancements in engineering, manufacturing, and transportation that revolutionized society and laid the groundwork for further scientific and technological progress. The innovations and developments of this era not only transformed industries and economies but also paved the way for the modern world of automation, mechanization, and interconnected global trade networks. The impact of industrialization on scientific research and technology continues to shape our world today, driving innovation and progress in diverse fields and contributing to the ongoing evolution of human society.

Key Developments in Engineering, Electricity, and Thermodynamics

Engineering has played a crucial role in shaping the modern world, with key advancements in the field revolutionizing industry, transportation, and infrastructure. Among the prominent figures in engineering history, James Watt stands out for his groundbreaking work on the steam engine. Watt's improvements to the steam engine in the late 18th century were instrumental in driving the Industrial Revolution, transforming the way power was generated and utilized in factories, mines, and transportation systems. By enhancing the efficiency and reliability of steam engines, Watt's innovations paved the way for significant advancements in industrial productivity and economic growth.

In the realm of electricity, Michael Faraday made significant contributions to the understanding of electromagnetism and the principles of electromagnetic induction. Faraday's experiments and discoveries in the early 19th century laid the foundation for the development of electric motors, generators, and transformers, which are essential components of modern electrical systems. His work also led to the concept of electromagnetic fields, which has had far-reaching implications in the fields of physics and engineering. Faraday's research on electricity and magnetism not only advanced scientific knowledge but also laid the groundwork for the practical applications of electromagnetic principles in various technologies.

Another pivotal figure in the field of electromagnetism is James Clerk Maxwell, whose electromagnetic theory provided a unified framework for understanding the interrelationship between electricity and magnetism. Maxwell's equations, formulated in the mid-19th century, described how electric and magnetic fields interact and propagate through space, leading to the prediction of electromagnetic waves. This theoretical framework not only confirmed the existence of light as an electromagnetic wave but also laid the foundation for the development of modern telecommunications, radio technology, and electromagnetic theory. Maxwell's contributions revolutionized the field of physics and set the stage for further advancements in the understanding of electromagnetism.

In the realm of thermodynamics, the study of heat and energy transfer, significant developments have been made that have shaped our understanding of energy conversion processes and the laws governing them. From the pioneering work of James Watt in improving the efficiency of steam engines to the formulation of the laws of thermodynamics by figures like Sadi Carnot and Rudolf Clausius, the field of thermodynamics has played a crucial role in the development of modern engineering and technology. The principles of thermodynamics have been instrumental in designing efficient power plants, engines, and refrigeration systems, contributing to advancements in energy production and utilization.

Overall, the contributions of Watt, Faraday, and Maxwell in the fields of engineering, electricity, and thermodynamics have had a profound impact on modern society, shaping the way we generate, utilize, and understand energy and technology. Their pioneering work has not only revolutionized industry and infrastructure but has also laid the foundation for further advancements in science and engineering, driving innovation and progress in the modern world.

The Birth of Modern Chemistry and the Periodic Table

Modern chemistry as a scientific discipline took shape in the 18th and 19th centuries, with significant contributions from pioneering chemists such as Antoine Lavoisier, John Dalton, and Dmitri Mendeleev. One of the most notable advancements in the field was the creation of the periodic table by Mendeleev, a Russian chemist, in the late 19th century. Mendeleev's work revolutionized the organization of chemical elements and provided a framework for understanding the properties and relationships of different elements.

Dmitri Mendeleev's development of the periodic table was a culmination of years of research and experimentation in the field of chemistry. In 1869, Mendeleev published his periodic table, which arranged the known chemical elements in order of increasing atomic mass and grouped elements with similar properties together. This arrangement allowed Mendeleev to predict the properties of undiscovered elements and identify gaps in the table where new elements were yet to be discovered.

Mendeleev's periodic table was a significant breakthrough in chemistry for several reasons. First, it provided a systematic way to organize the elements based on their atomic structure and properties, allowing chemists to better understand the relationships between different elements. Second, Mendeleev's table highlighted the periodicity of chemical properties, showing that elements exhibited recurring patterns in their properties when arranged in a certain order.

One of the key features of Mendeleev's periodic table was the concept of periodic law, which states that the properties of elements are periodic functions of their atomic numbers. This idea helped explain why certain elements exhibited similar chemical behaviors and why elements in the same group or period shared common characteristics.

Mendeleev's periodic table also had predictive power, as he was able to accurately predict the properties of several undiscovered elements based on the gaps in the table. When these elements were subsequently discovered and their properties matched Mendeleev's predictions, it provided strong evidence for the validity of his periodic table.

The development of the periodic table by Mendeleev laid the foundation for modern chemistry and our understanding of the behavior of chemical elements. It has since undergone refinements and expansions with the discovery of new elements and advancements in atomic theory, but Mendeleev's original work remains a cornerstone of the field.

In conclusion, the creation of the periodic table by Dmitri Mendeleev was a pivotal moment in the history of chemistry. By organizing the elements based on their atomic properties and predicting the existence and properties of undiscovered elements, Mendeleev's periodic table revolutionized the way we study and understand the building blocks of matter. His work continues to influence modern chemistry and serves as a testament to the power of scientific inquiry and innovation in shaping our understanding of the natural world.

Chapter 8

The 19th Century: Expanding Horizons

Advances in Biology and the Theory of Evolution

In the 19th century, a monumental shift occurred in the field of biology with the introduction of Charles Darwin's theory of evolution by natural selection. Darwin's groundbreaking work revolutionized our understanding of the natural world and laid the foundation for modern evolutionary biology. Alongside Darwin, Alfred Russel Wallace independently formulated similar ideas, leading to the co-presentation of the theory of evolution in 1858.

Darwin's theory of evolution posited that all species of life have descended from common ancestors through a process of natural selection. This mechanism of natural selection acts on variations within populations, favoring those traits that enhance an individual's survival and reproductive success. Over time, these advantageous traits become more prevalent in a population, leading to the gradual evolution of species.

One of the key aspects of Darwin's theory was the concept of adaptation – the idea that organisms are well-suited to their environments due to the accumulation of beneficial traits over successive generations. This idea challenged prevailing beliefs in fixed species and provided a unifying explanation for the diversity of life on Earth.

Alfred Russel Wallace, a contemporary of Darwin, independently arrived at similar conclusions regarding evolution by natural selection. Wallace's work in the Malay Archipelago and South America led him to propose a theory of evolution that closely mirrored Darwin's ideas. The joint publication of their findings in the Linnean Society of London marked a significant moment in the history of biological science.

The theory of evolution had profound implications for biology, ecology, and anthropology. It provided a framework for understanding the interconnectedness of all living organisms and the processes shaping biodiversity. Evolutionary principles have since been applied across various disciplines, from genetics and paleontology to conservation biology and medicine.

Darwin's theory of evolution continues to be a cornerstone of modern biology, supported by a wealth of empirical evidence from fields such as genetics, comparative anatomy, and biogeography. The discovery of DNA and the development of molecular biology have further bolstered our understanding of evolutionary processes, confirming the patterns of descent and genetic inheritance predicted by Darwin and Wallace.

In conclusion, the advances in biology and the theory of evolution ushered in a new era of scientific inquiry, transforming our understanding of the natural world and our place within it. Darwin and Wallace's contributions to the theory of evolution remain among the most influential ideas in the history of science, shaping our perception of life's diversity and interconnectedness. The evolutionary paradigm continues to inspire research and exploration, shedding light on the mechanisms driving the evolution of species and the remarkable diversity of life on Earth.

The Unification of Electromagnetism and the Study of Light

In the 19th century, significant advancements were made in the field of electromagnetism and the study of light, leading to a deeper understanding of the fundamental forces governing the natural world. This period marked a crucial turning point in the history of science, with groundbreaking contributions from scientists like James Clerk Maxwell and Heinrich Hertz.

James Clerk Maxwell, a Scottish physicist, played a pivotal role in unifying the previously separate fields of electricity and magnetism. Maxwell's equations, formulated in the mid-19th century, provided a comprehensive mathematical framework to describe the behavior of electromagnetic fields. These equations established the foundation for the field of classical electromagnetism and paved the way for the development of modern physics.

Maxwell's equations consist of a set of four fundamental equations that describe how electric and magnetic fields interact and propagate through space. These equations include Gauss's law for electricity, Gauss's law for magnetism, Faraday's law of electromagnetic induction, and Ampère's law with Maxwell's addition. Together, these equations quantitatively describe the relationships between electric charges, electric fields, magnetic fields, and electromagnetic waves.

Heinrich Hertz, a German physicist, conducted pioneering experiments in the late 19th century that confirmed the existence of electromagnetic waves predicted by Maxwell's equations. Hertz's experiments demonstrated the generation, transmission, and reception of electromagnetic waves, providing experimental validation of Maxwell's theoretical framework.

One of Hertz's most famous experiments involved the generation of electromagnetic waves using a spark oscillator and a simple antenna. By detecting these waves with a receiver consisting of a loop of wire with a small spark gap, Hertz was able to demonstrate the properties of electromagnetic radiation, including reflection, refraction, diffraction, and polarization.

Hertz's work not only confirmed the existence of electromagnetic waves but also laid the foundation for the development of wireless communication technologies that would revolutionize the modern world. His experiments marked a crucial step towards the practical application of electromagnetic waves for telecommunication, broadcasting, and other wireless technologies.

Overall, the unification of electromagnetism and the study of light during the 19th century represented a significant milestone in the history of science. The work of Maxwell and Hertz not only expanded our understanding of the fundamental forces of nature but also paved the way for the development of modern physics and technology. Their contributions continue to influence scientific research and technological innovation to this day, shaping the way we perceive and interact with the world around us.

The Beginnings of Modern Medicine and Microbiology

In the 19th century, the field of medicine underwent a profound transformation with the groundbreaking work of Louis Pasteur and Robert Koch, two pioneers who revolutionized our understanding of infectious diseases and laid the foundation for modern microbiology.

Louis Pasteur, a French chemist and microbiologist, is best known for his development of the germ theory of disease. Prior to Pasteur's work, it was commonly believed that diseases were caused by spontaneous generation or miasma (bad air). However, Pasteur's experiments demonstrated that microorganisms were responsible for the spread of diseases. He famously disproved the theory of spontaneous generation through his experiments with swan-necked flasks, showing that microorganisms in the air were the cause of contamination. This discovery had profound implications for medicine and led to the development of aseptic techniques in surgery and the concept of sterilization to prevent infections.

Pasteur's work also extended to the field of vaccination. He developed vaccines for several diseases, including anthrax and rabies. His development of the rabies vaccine was a significant breakthrough in preventive medicine and laid the groundwork for the field of immunology.

Robert Koch, a German physician and microbiologist, is renowned for his contributions to the identification of specific disease-causing bacteria. Koch formulated a set of postulates, now known as Koch's postulates, which are used to establish a causal relationship between a microorganism and a disease. He applied these postulates to identify the causative agents of diseases such as tuberculosis, cholera, and anthrax.

One of Koch's most notable achievements was the discovery of the bacterium Mycobacterium tuberculosis as the causative agent of tuberculosis. His work on tuberculosis not only led to the development of effective treatments for the disease but also laid the groundwork for the field of medical bacteriology.

Koch's research also played a crucial role in the field of epidemiology. By identifying the specific pathogens responsible for infectious diseases, Koch helped shape our understanding of how diseases spread and provided a scientific basis for the control and prevention of epidemics.

In summary, the contributions of Louis Pasteur and Robert Koch to the field of medicine and microbiology were transformative. Their work on germ theory, identification of disease-causing bacteria, and development of vaccines and diagnostic techniques revolutionized the practice of medicine and laid the groundwork for modern healthcare practices. Through their pioneering research, Pasteur and Koch ushered in a new era of scientific inquiry that continues to shape our understanding of infectious diseases and the principles of public health to this day.

Chapter 9

The Early 20th Century: Revolutionary Ideas

The Development of Quantum Mechanics and Relativity

The early 20th century marked a revolutionary period in the field of physics with the development of quantum mechanics and the theory of relativity. Albert Einstein's theory of relativity, particularly the special and general theories, reshaped our understanding of space, time, and gravity. Einstein's special theory of relativity, proposed in 1905, introduced the concept of spacetime and the famous equation $E=mc^2$, which demonstrated the equivalence of mass and energy. This theory fundamentally altered our understanding of the nature of light, time dilation, and the relationship between energy and mass.

In parallel with Einstein's work on relativity, quantum mechanics emerged as a new framework to understand the behavior of particles on a subatomic scale. Quantum mechanics challenged classical physics by introducing principles such as wave-particle duality and the uncertainty principle. Danish physicist Niels Bohr played a key role in the development of quantum theory with his atomic model, which incorporated discrete energy levels for electrons around the nucleus. Bohr's model provided a foundation for understanding the spectral lines of elements and laid the groundwork for future quantum mechanical theories.

German physicist Werner Heisenberg further advanced quantum mechanics with his uncertainty principle, which posited that the position and momentum of a particle cannot be precisely determined simultaneously. Heisenberg's work highlighted the probabilistic nature of quantum mechanics and the limitations of classical physics in describing the behavior of particles at the atomic level. Heisenberg's matrix mechanics and the wave function formalism developed by Erwin Schrödinger provided mathematical tools to describe the behavior of quantum systems and predict their properties.

The development of quantum mechanics and relativity revolutionized our understanding of the fundamental laws of nature and paved the way for modern physics. These theories not only explained observable phenomena at the subatomic scale but also had profound implications for technology, including the development of quantum computing, lasers, and nuclear energy. Quantum mechanics and relativity continue to drive research in physics, shaping our understanding of the universe at both the smallest and largest scales.

In conclusion, the development of quantum mechanics by physicists such as Bohr and Heisenberg, alongside Einstein's theory of relativity, represents a pivotal moment in the history of science. These groundbreaking theories challenged traditional scientific paradigms and opened up new avenues for exploration and discovery. The interplay between quantum mechanics and relativity continues to inspire researchers to push the boundaries of knowledge and explore the mysteries of the universe.

Advances in Genetics and the Discovery of DNA

Genetics, the study of heredity and variation in living organisms, underwent a revolutionary transformation in the early 20th century with the pioneering work of Gregor Mendel on inheritance patterns and the groundbreaking discovery of the structure of DNA by James Watson and Francis Crick. These advancements laid the foundation for modern genetics and molecular biology, reshaping our understanding of how traits are passed down from generation to generation.

Gregor Mendel, an Austrian monk, conducted experiments on pea plants in the mid-19th century and formulated the laws of inheritance that became the basis of classical genetics. Mendel's work demonstrated the principles of segregation and independent assortment of genes, revealing the mechanisms by which traits are inherited from parents to offspring. His discoveries provided a framework for understanding genetic inheritance and set the stage for further exploration into the molecular basis of heredity.

In the early 1950s, James Watson, an American biologist, and Francis Crick, a British physicist, made one of the most significant breakthroughs in the history of science by elucidating the structure of DNA. Building upon the research of Rosalind Franklin and Maurice Wilkins, who provided crucial X-ray diffraction data of DNA, Watson and Crick proposed the double helix model of DNA in 1953. Their model depicted DNA as a twisted ladder-like structure composed of two strands of nucleotides held together by hydrogen bonds between complementary base pairs (adenine-thymine and guanine-cytosine).

The discovery of the DNA double helix was a monumental achievement with far-reaching implications for genetics, biochemistry, and molecular biology. It revealed the molecular basis of heredity and provided insights into how genetic information is stored, replicated, and transmitted in living organisms. The complementary base pairing of nucleotides allowed for the faithful replication of DNA during cell division and served as the template for protein synthesis through the genetic code.

Moreover, the elucidation of the DNA structure facilitated the understanding of how mutations, genetic variations, and genetic diseases arise. It paved the way for the field of molecular genetics, enabling scientists to study the mechanisms of gene expression, regulation, and genetic disorders at the molecular level. The discovery of DNA also led to the development of techniques such as polymerase chain reaction (PCR), DNA sequencing, and genetic engineering, which have revolutionized biomedical research and biotechnology.

In conclusion, the advances in genetics through Mendel's laws of inheritance and the discovery of the DNA structure by Watson and Crick have had a profound impact on our understanding of heredity, evolution, and the molecular basis of life. These breakthroughs have transformed the field of genetics, opening up new avenues for research and applications in medicine, agriculture, and biotechnology. The study of genetics continues to unravel the complexities of the genetic code and holds great promise for future discoveries in understanding and manipulating the genetic information that shapes all living organisms.

Innovations in Technology and Applied Science

Innovations in Technology and Applied Science have played a significant role in shaping the modern world, with key figures such as Thomas Edison, Nikola Tesla, and Guglielmo Marconi making groundbreaking contributions that revolutionized various aspects of technology and communication.

Thomas Edison, often referred to as the "Wizard of Menlo Park," is credited with inventing the first commercially viable electric light bulb. In 1879, after years of experimentation and refinement, Edison successfully created a practical incandescent light bulb that could be mass-produced and used for lighting homes, streets, and businesses. This invention had a profound impact on society, ushering in a new era of illumination and transforming the way people lived and worked by extending the hours of productivity and leisure activities.

Nikola Tesla, a brilliant Serbian-American inventor and electrical engineer, is known for his pioneering work in the development of alternating current (AC) electrical systems. Tesla's inventions and contributions to the field of electricity and magnetism were instrumental in the advancement of power generation, transmission, and distribution. His development of the polyphase AC system laid the foundation for the modern electrical grid and enabled the efficient distribution of electricity over long distances. Tesla's innovations in AC technology revolutionized the way electricity was harnessed and utilized, facilitating the widespread adoption of electric power in homes, industries, and transportation.

Guglielmo Marconi, an Italian inventor and entrepreneur, is recognized as the father of modern wireless communication. In the late 19th and early 20th centuries, Marconi conducted groundbreaking experiments in wireless telegraphy and successfully transmitted radio signals across long distances without the need for physical wires. His invention of the wireless telegraph and the establishment of the first transatlantic radio communication link marked a significant milestone in the development of global communication systems. Marconi's work laid the foundation for the evolution of radio broadcasting, maritime communication, and later developments in wireless telephony and internet communication technologies.

The inventions and contributions of Edison, Tesla, and Marconi not only revolutionized technology and communication but also had far-reaching implications for society, economy, and culture. These innovators exemplify the spirit of scientific inquiry, experimentation, and ingenuity that drives progress and innovation in the field of technology and applied science. Their pioneering work continues to inspire future generations of inventors, engineers, and scientists to push the boundaries of knowledge and creativity in pursuit of transformative advancements that shape the world we live in today.

Chapter 10

The Mid to Late 20th Century: Science Transformed

The Space Race and the Exploration of the Cosmos

The Space Race and the Exploration of the Cosmos was a pivotal era in the history of science, characterized by fierce competition between the United States' NASA and the Soviet space program. This chapter highlights the remarkable achievements that marked this period, including the historic moon landing and groundbreaking interplanetary probes.

One of the most iconic events of the Space Race was the Apollo 11 mission, which culminated in the first human landing on the moon on July 20, 1969. Astronauts Neil Armstrong and Buzz Aldrin became the first humans to set foot on another celestial body, while Michael Collins orbited above in the command module. This monumental achievement not only demonstrated the technological prowess of the United States but also symbolized a giant leap for humankind in its quest to explore the cosmos.

The success of the Apollo program was built upon earlier missions, such as Mercury and Gemini, which laid the groundwork for human spaceflight and orbital rendezvous. These missions tested the capabilities of spacecraft and astronauts, paving the way for the ambitious goal of landing on the moon.

Meanwhile, the Soviet space program made significant contributions to space exploration, including launching the first artificial satellite, Sputnik, in 1957, and sending the first human, Yuri Gagarin, into space in 1961. The Soviet Union also achieved milestones like the first spacewalk and the first successful soft landing on the moon with the Luna program.

Interplanetary probes were another key aspect of the Space Race, as both the United States and the Soviet Union sought to explore and study other celestial bodies in our solar system. The Mariner and Voyager missions launched by NASA provided unprecedented insights into the planets of our solar system, capturing stunning images and collecting valuable scientific data. Similarly, the Soviet Venera probes conducted successful missions to Venus, revealing the harsh conditions of the planet's atmosphere.

The Space Race not only fueled advancements in space technology but also inspired generations of scientists, engineers, and explorers. It showcased the power of human ingenuity and determination in pushing the boundaries of what was thought possible in space exploration.

The collaboration and competition between NASA and the Soviet space program during the Space Race led to a rapid acceleration of space exploration capabilities and knowledge. It laid the foundation for future missions to Mars, the outer planets, and beyond, shaping our understanding of the cosmos and our place within it.

In conclusion, the Space Race and the Exploration of the Cosmos marked a transformative period in the history of science, where bold visions and daring missions reshaped our understanding of the universe. The achievements of NASA and the Soviet space program during this era continue to inspire and drive the pursuit of new frontiers in space exploration.

Developments in Computer Science and Information Technology

Computer science and information technology have revolutionized the way we live, work, and communicate in the modern world. This section delves into the significant contributions of two pioneers in the field – Alan Turing and John von Neumann – whose work laid the foundation for the development of computer science and computer architecture as we know it today.

Alan Turing, a British mathematician, logician, and cryptanalyst, is widely regarded as one of the founding fathers of computer science. Turing's most notable achievement was his conceptualization of the Turing machine, a theoretical device that laid the groundwork for modern computing. The Turing machine introduced the concept of a universal machine capable of performing any computation that could be described algorithmically. This idea formed the basis of the stored-program computer, where instructions and data are stored in the computer's memory, allowing for versatile and programmable computation.

Turing's wartime code-breaking work at Bletchley Park during World War II, where he played a crucial role in cracking the German Enigma code, showcased the practical applications of his theoretical work. His pioneering efforts in developing the bombe machine to decipher encrypted messages significantly influenced the field of cryptography and laid the groundwork for modern information security protocols.

On the other hand, John von Neumann, a Hungarian-American mathematician and physicist, made key contributions to the design and architecture of modern computers. Von Neumann's most significant achievement was his design of the von Neumann architecture, which outlined the fundamental structure of a stored-program computer. In this architecture, instructions and data are stored in the same memory, allowing for the seamless execution of programs and the manipulation of data by the central processing unit (CPU).

The von Neumann architecture introduced the concept of a computer with a central processing unit, memory, input/output devices, and a control unit – a design that has become the standard model for digital computers. Von Neumann's work not only revolutionized the field of computer architecture but also laid the groundwork for the development of high-level programming languages and operating systems.

Together, Turing and von Neumann's contributions formed the basis of modern computer science and information technology. Their innovative ideas and theoretical frameworks paved the way for the development of electronic computers, which have since become indispensable tools in various fields, including scientific research, business operations, communication, and entertainment.

In conclusion, the enduring legacies of Alan Turing and John von Neumann in the realms of computer science and information technology highlight the transformative power of their ideas and innovations. Their pioneering work continues to shape the technological landscape and drive advancements in computing, artificial intelligence, data processing, and beyond.

Breakthroughs in Medical Science and Biotechnology

Breakthroughs in Medical Science and Biotechnology have revolutionized the field of healthcare and have had a profound impact on human health and well-being. In this section, we will explore three significant advancements: Salk's polio vaccine, Pauling's work on molecular biology, and the Human Genome Project.

1. Salk's Polio Vaccine: One of the most significant breakthroughs in medical history was the development of the polio vaccine by Dr. Jonas Salk in the mid-20th century. Polio, a highly infectious viral disease, had caused widespread fear and devastation, particularly affecting children. Salk's vaccine, which was based on inactivated poliovirus, was a monumental achievement in the field of immunization. The successful deployment of the polio vaccine led to a dramatic decrease in polio cases globally and eventually paved the way for the near eradication of the disease. Salk's work not only saved countless lives but also demonstrated the power of vaccination in preventing infectious diseases.

2. Pauling's Work on Molecular Biology: Linus Pauling, a renowned chemist and biologist, made significant contributions to the field of molecular biology. Pauling's groundbreaking research on the structure of proteins and nucleic acids laid the foundation for our understanding of the molecular basis of life. His work on the nature of chemical bonds and the structure of complex molecules, such as DNA, provided crucial insights into the fundamental processes underlying biological systems. Pauling's discoveries have had a lasting impact on fields ranging from genetics to biochemistry and have shaped our understanding of the molecular mechanisms that govern life.

3. The Human Genome Project: The Human Genome Project, a collaborative scientific initiative launched in the late 20th century, aimed to map and sequence the entire human genome. This ambitious undertaking involved scientists from around the world working together to decode the genetic blueprint of human beings. The completion of the Human Genome Project marked a major milestone in genetics and biotechnology, providing researchers with a wealth of information about the structure and function of human genes. The project has revolutionized the fields of genomics and personalized medicine, leading to insights into genetic diseases, drug development, and the understanding of human evolution.

In conclusion, the breakthroughs in medical science and biotechnology highlighted in this section have had a transformative impact on healthcare and scientific research. From the development of life-saving vaccines to the unraveling of the genetic code, these advancements have advanced our understanding of human biology and disease mechanisms. The pioneering work of individuals like Salk, Pauling, and the collaborative efforts of the Human Genome Project have paved the way for innovations in medicine and biotechnology that continue to shape the future of healthcare and scientific discovery.

Chapter 11

Contemporary Science and Future Directions

Modern Advancements in Physics and Cosmology

Modern Advancements in Physics and Cosmology have seen significant progress in recent years, pushing the boundaries of our understanding of the universe. Two key areas of breakthroughs have been the discovery of the Higgs boson and advancements in black hole research.

The discovery of the Higgs boson, also known as the "God particle," was a major milestone in particle physics. The Higgs boson is a fundamental particle that is crucial to the understanding of how particles acquire mass. The existence of the Higgs boson was predicted by the Standard Model of particle physics, which is the framework that describes the fundamental particles and their interactions. In 2012, scientists at CERN's Large Hadron Collider announced the discovery of a particle consistent with the Higgs boson, confirming one of the last missing pieces of the Standard Model. This discovery provided crucial validation of our understanding of particle physics and the mechanism by which particles acquire mass.

Advancements in black hole research have also been groundbreaking in recent years. Black holes are regions of spacetime with such strong gravitational effects that nothing, not even light, can escape from them. The study of black holes has been a key focus in astrophysics and cosmology, with new observations and theoretical developments shedding light on these mysterious cosmic entities. In 2019, the Event Horizon Telescope collaboration made history by capturing the first-ever image of a black hole. The image, which showed the silhouette of the supermassive black hole at the center of the galaxy M87, provided direct observational evidence of these enigmatic objects.

Furthermore, research on black holes has led to discoveries related to their properties, behavior, and interactions with their surrounding environments. Scientists have studied the dynamics of black hole accretion disks, the emission of powerful jets of particles from black hole regions, and the gravitational waves produced by the mergers of black holes. These studies have not only deepened our understanding of black holes but have also provided insights into the fundamental nature of gravity and spacetime.

In addition to the Higgs boson and black hole research, advancements in cosmology have also played a significant role in shaping our understanding of the universe. Observations from telescopes and satellites have revealed new insights into the composition, structure, and evolution of the cosmos. Discoveries such as dark matter, dark energy, cosmic microwave background radiation, and the large-scale structure of the universe have all contributed to our current cosmological model.

Overall, the modern advancements in physics and cosmology represent a vibrant and dynamic field of research that continues to push the boundaries of scientific knowledge. The discovery of the Higgs boson and advancements in black hole research have opened new avenues for exploration and have paved the way for further discoveries that will deepen our understanding of the fundamental laws governing the universe.

Cutting-Edge Research in Genetics, Nanotechnology, and AI

In the modern era, cutting-edge research in genetics, nanotechnology, and artificial intelligence (AI) has pushed the boundaries of scientific discovery and technological innovation to unprecedented levels. These fields represent the forefront of scientific exploration, offering immense potential for revolutionizing various aspects of human life and society.

Genetics, once considered a mysterious realm of inheritance and biological diversity, has now become a realm of precise manipulation and modification through breakthrough technologies like CRISPR gene editing. CRISPR-Cas9 is a revolutionary tool that enables scientists to precisely edit genetic sequences with unprecedented accuracy and efficiency. This technology has opened up new possibilities in treating genetic disorders, creating genetically modified organisms, and understanding the fundamental mechanisms of life at the molecular level. The ability to edit genes with such precision holds promise for addressing previously incurable diseases and developing targeted therapies tailored to an individual's genetic makeup.

Nanotechnology, the science of manipulating materials at the atomic and molecular scale, has also witnessed remarkable advancements in recent years. Nanotechnology applications span a wide range of fields, from medicine and electronics to energy and environmental sustainability. Nanomaterials exhibit unique properties that can be harnessed for various purposes, such as targeted drug delivery systems in healthcare, ultra-efficient solar cells in renewable energy, and high-performance materials in aerospace and construction. The ability to engineer materials at the nanoscale opens up new avenues for innovation and the creation of novel technologies with unprecedented capabilities.

Artificial intelligence (AI) has emerged as a transformative force in the realm of technology, enabling machines to perform tasks that traditionally required human intelligence. AI systems are capable of learning, reasoning, and making decisions autonomously, revolutionizing industries such as healthcare, finance, transportation, and entertainment. Machine learning algorithms, neural networks, and deep learning models have propelled AI to new heights, enabling applications like autonomous vehicles, natural language processing, and personalized recommendations. The rise of AI has the potential to reshape the way we live and work, offering solutions to complex problems and unlocking new opportunities for innovation and efficiency.

The convergence of genetics, nanotechnology, and AI holds promise for interdisciplinary collaboration and synergistic advancements. Integrating genetic insights with nanoscale technologies and AI-driven analytics can lead to personalized medicine approaches, smart materials with adaptive capabilities, and intelligent systems that enhance human capabilities. These interdisciplinary endeavors have the potential to revolutionize healthcare, manufacturing, information technology, and many other sectors, paving the way for a future where science and technology work hand in hand to address global challenges and improve the quality of life for all.

As we look to the future, the continued progress in genetics, nanotechnology, and AI promises to unlock new frontiers of scientific exploration and technological innovation. By harnessing the power of these cutting-edge fields, researchers and innovators can shape a world where the boundaries of what is possible are constantly expanding, driving us towards a future filled with endless possibilities and opportunities for growth and advancement.

The Role of Science in Addressing Global Challenges

Science plays a crucial role in addressing some of the most pressing global challenges facing humanity today. Three key areas where science is instrumental in making a positive impact are in tackling climate change, developing renewable energy sources, and improving public health.

Climate Change:
One of the most significant challenges facing the world is climate change, driven primarily by human activities such as burning fossil fuels, deforestation, and industrial processes. Science provides the tools and knowledge necessary to understand the causes and effects of climate change, as well as to develop solutions to mitigate its impacts. Through the collection and analysis of data, climate scientists can track

changes in temperature, sea levels, and weather patterns, providing valuable insights into the extent of global warming. Furthermore, scientific research helps in modeling future climate scenarios, allowing policymakers to make informed decisions on mitigation and adaptation strategies. Technologies such as renewable energy, carbon capture and storage, and sustainable land management practices all stem from scientific advancements aimed at reducing greenhouse gas emissions and transitioning to a low-carbon economy.

Renewable Energy Sources:
As the world seeks to move away from fossil fuels and towards cleaner, more sustainable energy sources, science is at the forefront of developing renewable energy technologies. Solar, wind, hydroelectric, and geothermal energy are all examples of renewable energy sources that rely on scientific principles for their harnessing and utilization. Scientists and engineers work to improve the efficiency and affordability of these technologies, making them viable alternatives to traditional fossil fuels. Research in materials science, energy storage, and grid integration are key areas where scientific innovation is driving the transition to a more sustainable energy future. By investing in renewable energy research and development, countries can reduce their carbon footprint, enhance energy security, and create new economic opportunities in the clean energy sector.

Improving Public Health:
Science also plays a vital role in improving public health outcomes around the world. From understanding the biology of diseases to developing vaccines, treatments, and public health interventions, scientific research is essential in combating infectious diseases, non-communicable diseases, and emerging health threats. Epidemiologists use mathematical modeling and

data analysis to track the spread of diseases and inform public health policies. Medical researchers work to develop new drugs, therapies, and medical technologies to treat and prevent illnesses. Furthermore, advancements in genomics, personalized medicine, and digital health technologies are revolutionizing healthcare delivery and improving patient outcomes. By investing in scientific research and public health infrastructure, countries can better respond to health crises, strengthen healthcare systems, and promote overall well-being in their populations.

In conclusion, the role of science in addressing global challenges cannot be overstated. From climate change to renewable energy to public health, scientific research and innovation are essential in finding sustainable solutions to complex problems. By supporting scientific endeavors, investing in research and development, and fostering international collaboration, we can harness the power of science to create a more resilient, equitable, and sustainable future for all.

Conclusion

Summary of the Evolution and Impact of Science Throughout History

The evolution and impact of science throughout history have been profound and far-reaching, shaping the course of human civilization and driving progress across various fields. From ancient times to the present day, science has played a crucial role in advancing human understanding, improving quality of life, and driving technological and cultural advancements.

Ancient civilizations such as Mesopotamia, Egypt, the Indus Valley, and China made significant contributions to science in areas such as astronomy, mathematics, medicine, engineering, and urban planning. The early Greek philosophers and scientists, including Thales, Pythagoras, and Aristotle, laid the foundation for Western scientific thought with their work in geometry, mathematics, music theory, biology, and physics.

The Classical period saw advancements in Hellenistic science with figures like Euclid, Archimedes, and Ptolemy making key contributions to mathematics, mechanics, astronomy, and geography. The Roman Empire furthered scientific knowledge through engineering feats, medical practices, and natural history studies.

The Islamic Golden Age marked a period of significant scientific progress with the translation movement and the establishment of the House of Wisdom in Baghdad. Scholars like Al-Khwarizmi,

Ibn Sina, and Alhazen made important contributions to mathematics, astronomy, medicine, and optics during this time.

Medieval Europe saw a revival of learning with the Carolingian Renaissance and the integration of Greek and Islamic science through figures like Thomas Aquinas and Roger Bacon. The Renaissance and Scientific Revolution further propelled scientific advancements with key figures like Copernicus, Galileo, Kepler, and Newton revolutionizing our understanding of the cosmos and laying the groundwork for modern scientific inquiry.

The Age of Enlightenment brought about a focus on empirical observation and the establishment of scientific societies and academies, fostering collaboration and communication among scientists. The Industrial Revolution spurred advancements in engineering, electricity, and chemistry, leading to the birth of modern science and the development of the periodic table.

The 19th and 20th centuries saw remarkable progress in biology, electromagnetism, genetics, quantum mechanics, relativity, technology, and space exploration. Breakthroughs in medicine, technology, and biotechnology further transformed scientific research and its applications in society.

In contemporary times, science continues to push the boundaries of knowledge with advancements in physics, cosmology, genetics, nanotechnology, and artificial intelligence. Science also plays a crucial role in addressing global challenges such as climate change, renewable energy, and public health.

In conclusion, the evolution of science has been a testament to human curiosity, ingenuity, and perseverance. The impact of science throughout history has been profound, shaping our understanding of the world and driving progress in all aspects of human life. As we look towards the future, the potential for further scientific advancements remains vast, offering endless possibilities for discovery and innovation.

Reflections on the Future of Scientific Discovery and Its Potential

In reflecting on the future of scientific discovery and its potential, it is essential to acknowledge the rapid pace at which advancements in science and technology are occurring. As we stand on the brink of a new era characterized by unprecedented connectivity, computational power, and interdisciplinary collaboration, the possibilities for scientific breakthroughs are virtually limitless. Here, we explore some key areas where future scientific research is poised to make significant contributions:

1. Interdisciplinary Collaboration: One of the most promising avenues for future scientific discovery lies in fostering collaboration across diverse fields such as biology, physics, computer science, and engineering. By breaking down traditional disciplinary boundaries, researchers can gain new insights and approaches to solving complex problems. For example, the integration of artificial intelligence with genomics has the potential to revolutionize personalized medicine and drug discovery.

2. Emerging Technologies: The development and application of emerging technologies like quantum computing, nanotechnology, and synthetic biology hold immense promise for driving scientific progress in the coming decades. Quantum computing, for instance, has the potential to revolutionize fields such as cryptography, materials science, and drug design by solving complex problems at speeds far beyond traditional computers.

3. Climate Change Mitigation and Sustainability: With the increasing urgency of addressing climate change and environmental degradation, future scientific research will play a crucial role in developing sustainable solutions. From renewable energy technologies to carbon capture and storage methods, scientists are at the forefront of finding innovative ways to mitigate the impact of human activities on the planet.

4. Health and Medicine: The field of healthcare is undergoing a transformation with the advent of precision medicine, gene editing technologies like CRISPR, and advancements in understanding the human microbiome. The future of medical research holds promise for personalized treatments, regenerative medicine, and innovative approaches to combating infectious diseases and chronic conditions.

5. Artificial Intelligence and Machine Learning: The integration of artificial intelligence and machine learning algorithms into various scientific disciplines has the potential to accelerate the pace of discovery and innovation. From drug discovery to climate modeling, AI-powered tools can analyze vast amounts of data, identify patterns, and make predictions that were previously unimaginable.

6. Space Exploration and Astrophysics: As humanity continues to push the boundaries of space exploration, future scientific research will focus on understanding the origins of the universe, exploring exoplanets for signs of life, and developing technologies for interplanetary travel. Advancements in space telescopes, propulsion systems, and robotics will enable new discoveries and expand our understanding of the cosmos.

In considering the future of scientific discovery, it is important to recognize the ethical and societal implications of emerging technologies. As scientists push the boundaries of knowledge and innovation, it is crucial to ensure that research is conducted responsibly, with careful consideration of potential risks and benefits to humanity and the environment.

Overall, the future of scientific discovery holds immense promise for addressing some of the most pressing challenges facing our world today. By fostering interdisciplinary collaboration, embracing emerging technologies, and maintaining a commitment to ethical and sustainable practices, scientists can unlock new frontiers of knowledge and pave the way for a brighter and more sustainable future for all.

Appendices

Timeline of Key Events in the History of Science

The timeline of key events in the history of science is a crucial aspect of understanding the evolution and impact of scientific knowledge throughout human history. This chronological list highlights significant scientific discoveries and developments that have shaped our understanding of the natural world and propelled technological advancements. Below is a detailed section on the timeline of key events in the history of science:

1. Prehistoric Times (10,000 BCE - 3,000 BCE)

- Early humans develop rudimentary tools and observe natural phenomena.
- Agricultural revolution leads to the domestication of plants and animals.

2. Ancient Mesopotamia (3500 BCE - 539 BCE)

- Babylonians develop advanced mathematical systems, including the concept of zero.
- Mesopotamian astronomers track celestial movements and create the first calendars.

3. Ancient Egypt (3100 BCE - 332 BCE)

- Egyptian physicians practice advanced medical techniques, such as surgery and dentistry.
- Construction of the Great Pyramid at Giza showcases engineering prowess.

4. Ancient Greece (800 BCE - 146 BCE)
   - Thales introduces principles of geometry and astronomy.
   - Pythagoras formulates mathematical theories, including the famous Pythagorean theorem.

5. Hellenistic Period (323 BCE - 31 BCE)
   - Euclid's "Elements" establishes the foundations of geometry.
   - Archimedes makes significant contributions to mechanics and hydrostatics.

6. Islamic Golden Age (8th - 14th centuries)
   - Al-Khwarizmi pioneers algebra and algorithms.
   - Alhazen's work on optics influences the scientific method.

7. European Renaissance (14th - 17th centuries)
   - Copernicus proposes heliocentrism, challenging the geocentric model.
   - Galileo's telescopic observations support the heliocentric theory.

8. Scientific Revolution (16th - 18th centuries)
   - Newton formulates laws of motion and universal gravitation.
   - Boyle's experiments lay the foundation for modern chemistry.

9. Industrial Revolution (18th - 19th centuries)
   - Watt's steam engine revolutionizes transportation and manufacturing.
   - Faraday's discoveries in electromagnetism pave the way for modern technology.

10. 20th Century (1900s)
   - Einstein's theory of relativity revolutionizes physics.
   - Watson and Crick discover the double helix structure of DNA.

11. Space Age (1950s - present)
   - NASA and Soviet space programs achieve significant milestones in space exploration.
   - Mars rovers and space telescopes expand our understanding of the cosmos.

12. Modern Era (21st century)
   - CRISPR gene editing technology offers new possibilities for genetic modification.
   - Advancements in artificial intelligence drive innovation in various fields.

This timeline of key events in the history of science showcases the continuous evolution of human knowledge and the profound impact of scientific discoveries on society. It underscores the importance of scientific inquiry in shaping our understanding of the world and driving progress in various fields.

Biographies of Notable Scientists and Their Contributions

1. Archimedes (c. 287-212 BC) - A Greek mathematician, physicist, engineer, and inventor, Archimedes is known for his contributions to the fields of geometry and mechanics. He is credited with discovering the principles of buoyancy and the lever, as well as developing the concept of pi. His work laid the foundation for modern physics and engineering.

2. Ibn Sina (Avicenna) (980-1037) - A Persian polymath, Ibn Sina made significant contributions to medicine, philosophy, astronomy, and mathematics. His most famous work, "The Canon of Medicine," was a comprehensive medical encyclopedia that influenced medical practice in both the East and the West for centuries. He also made advancements in the field of optics and astronomy.

3. Nicolaus Copernicus (1473-1543) - A Polish astronomer, Copernicus proposed the heliocentric model of the universe, challenging the prevailing geocentric view. His groundbreaking work, "De Revolutionibus Orbium Coelestium," laid the foundation for modern astronomy and revolutionized our understanding of the cosmos.

4. Marie Curie (1867-1934) - A pioneering physicist and chemist, Marie Curie was the first woman to win a Nobel Prize and remains the only person to have won Nobel Prizes in two different scientific fields (Physics and Chemistry). Her research on radioactivity led to the discovery of the elements polonium and radium, and her work laid the groundwork for advancements in nuclear physics and medicine.

5. Albert Einstein (1879-1955) - One of the most renowned physicists in history, Albert Einstein is best known for his theory of relativity, which revolutionized our understanding of space, time, and gravity. He also made significant contributions to quantum mechanics and cosmology, earning him the Nobel Prize in Physics in 1921.

6. Rosalind Franklin (1920-1958) - An English chemist and X-ray crystallographer, Rosalind Franklin played a crucial role in the discovery of the structure of DNA. Her work provided key insights that were instrumental in the development of the double helix model of DNA, though her contributions were often overshadowed by her male colleagues.

7. Stephen Hawking (1942-2018) - A theoretical physicist and cosmologist, Stephen Hawking made groundbreaking contributions to our understanding of black holes, the nature of the universe, and the concept of time. Despite being diagnosed with a debilitating motor neuron disease at a young age, Hawking's work continues to inspire scientists and the general public alike.

8. Jane Goodall (1934-present) - A British primatologist and conservationist, Jane Goodall is renowned for her groundbreaking research on chimpanzees in Tanzania. Her work revolutionized our understanding of primate behavior and highlighted the importance of conservation efforts to protect endangered species and their habitats.

9. Carl Sagan (1934-1996) - An American astronomer, cosmologist, and science communicator, Carl Sagan popularized science through his books, television series, and public lectures. He played a key role in advancing our understanding of the cosmos and advocating for scientific literacy and critical thinking.

10. Jennifer Doudna (1964-present) - An American biochemist, Jennifer Doudna co-discovered the CRISPR-Cas9 gene editing technology, a revolutionary tool that has transformed genetic research and holds immense potential for applications in medicine, agriculture, and biotechnology. Her work has paved the way for new avenues in precision genetic engineering.

These brief biographies highlight the diverse contributions of influential scientists throughout history, showcasing their lasting impact on scientific knowledge and innovation.

Glossary of Scientific Terms and Concepts

The Glossary of Scientific Terms and Concepts serves as a valuable resource for readers to understand and grasp the important terminology and concepts discussed throughout 'The History of Science.' This comprehensive glossary provides definitions and explanations of key scientific terms and concepts to aid in the comprehension of the intricate scientific developments and contributions highlighted in the book.

1. Science: The systematic study of the natural world through observation, experimentation, and reasoning to understand the underlying principles governing various phenomena.

2. Scientific Method: A systematic approach to scientific inquiry involving observation, hypothesis formation, experimentation, and analysis to test and refine theories and understand natural phenomena.

3. Empirical Observation: The practice of gathering information through sensory perception and direct experience to form the basis of scientific knowledge.

4. Natural Philosophy: The precursor to modern science, focusing on philosophical inquiry into the natural world and its phenomena based on observation and reason.

5. Astronomy: The study of celestial objects, their movements, and the physical laws governing the universe.

6. Mathematics: The field of study dealing with numbers, quantities, shapes, and patterns, used to describe and explain the relationships between various phenomena.

7. Engineering: The application of scientific and mathematical principles to design, develop, and optimize structures, systems, and processes to meet human needs.

8. Medicine: The branch of science focused on the diagnosis, treatment, and prevention of diseases and disorders to promote human health and well-being.

9. Biology: The study of living organisms and their interactions with each other and their environment, encompassing various subfields such as genetics, evolution, and ecology.

10. Physics: The branch of science concerned with the fundamental principles governing matter, energy, motion, and forces in the universe.

11. Chemistry: The study of the composition, properties, and interactions of substances and the transformations they undergo, forming the basis of modern chemical knowledge.

12. Geology: The study of the Earth's physical structure, composition, and processes, including the formation of rocks, minerals, and geological features.

13. Optics: The branch of physics dealing with the behavior of light, its properties, and its interactions with matter.

14. Electromagnetism: The scientific theory describing the relationship between electricity and magnetism, encompassing phenomena such as electromagnetic waves and fields.

15. Genetics: The study of heredity and variation in living organisms, focusing on genes, DNA, and genetic inheritance patterns.

16. Evolution: The process of change in living organisms over time, driven by natural selection and genetic variation, as proposed by Charles Darwin.

17. Quantum Mechanics: The branch of physics dealing with the behavior of particles at the atomic and subatomic levels, characterized by probabilistic outcomes and wave-particle duality.

18. Relativity: The theory proposed by Albert Einstein describing the relationships between space, time, and gravity, including special and general relativity.

19. Biotechnology: The use of living organisms, cells, and biological systems to develop products and technologies for various applications, including medicine, agriculture, and industry.

20. Artificial Intelligence: The development of computer systems capable of performing tasks that typically require human intelligence, such as learning, problem-solving, and decision-making.

This glossary provides a foundational understanding of the diverse scientific terms and concepts discussed in the book, enabling readers to delve deeper into the historical developments and advancements in science from ancient times to the modern era. By familiarizing themselves with these essential terms, readers can enhance their comprehension and appreciation of the significant contributions of science to human progress and knowledge.

Bibliography and Further Reading

For readers interested in delving deeper into the history of science and exploring the vast array of scientific discoveries and developments, there are numerous authoritative sources and additional reading materials available. Below is a curated list of key texts and references that provide comprehensive insights into the evolution and impact of science throughout history:

1. "The Structure of Scientific Revolutions" by Thomas S. Kuhn - This seminal work explores the concept of scientific revolutions and paradigm shifts, offering a critical analysis of how scientific knowledge advances over time.

2. "A Short History of Nearly Everything" by Bill Bryson - A captivating narrative that covers a wide range of scientific topics, from the origins of the universe to the development of modern scientific disciplines.

3. "Sapiens: A Brief History of Humankind" by Yuval Noah Harari - While not solely focused on science, this book offers a thought-provoking exploration of the history of humanity and the role of science in shaping our understanding of the world.

4. "The Discoverers" by Daniel J. Boorstin - A comprehensive overview of the history of scientific exploration and discovery, spanning from ancient civilizations to the modern era.

5. "The Age of Wonder: How the Romantic Generation Discovered the Beauty and Terror of Science" by Richard Holmes - This book delves into the intersection of science and art during the Romantic era, highlighting the groundbreaking discoveries and innovations of the period.

6. "The Making of the Atomic Bomb" by Richard Rhodes - A detailed account of the development of nuclear physics and the race to build the atomic bomb during World War II, shedding light on the profound impact of science on society.

7. "Longitude: The True Story of a Lone Genius Who Solved the Greatest Scientific Problem of His Time" by Dava Sobel - An engaging narrative that explores the history of navigation and the quest to determine longitude at sea, showcasing the ingenuity and perseverance of scientific pioneers.

8. "The Elegant Universe: Superstrings, Hidden Dimensions, and the Quest for the Ultimate Theory" by Brian Greene - A fascinating exploration of modern theoretical physics, including concepts such as string theory and the quest for a unified theory of everything.

9. "The Emperor of All Maladies: A Biography of Cancer" by Siddhartha Mukherjee - A compelling account of the history of cancer research and treatment, illustrating the complex interplay between science, medicine, and society.

10. "The Gene: An Intimate History" by Siddhartha Mukherjee - This book provides a comprehensive overview of the history of genetics, from Mendel's experiments to the modern era of gene editing and personalized medicine.

These recommended readings offer a diverse and engaging perspective on the history of science, spanning a wide range of scientific disciplines and historical periods. Whether you are a newcomer to the subject or a seasoned enthusiast, these texts provide valuable insights and a deeper understanding of the evolution and impact of science throughout human history.

Share Your Thoughts!

Dear Valued Reader,

Thank you for reading our history of science book. This book is brought to you by **Skriuwer**, a group dedicated to creating interesting and easy-to-read content. Our goal is to take you through the exciting history of science, from its ancient beginnings to its significant impact on the world today.

We hope you enjoyed the stories and important moments we gathered for you. Our aim is to give you a book that not only teaches but also shares the remarkable journey of scientific discovery, showing how it has evolved, explored, and influenced history.

Your journey doesn't have to end now that you've finished the book. We see you as a key part of our community. If you have any comments, questions, or ideas on how we can make this book better or what we should write about next, please reach out to us at **kontakt@skriuwer.com**. Your feedback is very helpful and helps us create better content for you and others.

Did the history keep you interested and help you learn more about science? Please leave a review where you bought the book. Your thoughts not only inspire us but also help other readers find and choose this book.

Thank you for choosing **Skriuwer**. Let's keep exploring the fascinating history of science together.

With Thanks,
The Skriuwer Team

Printed in Great Britain
by Amazon